BURTON OF BEVERLEY

Pictures of Beverley and District by Thomas Bonfrey Burton 1866-1941

Edited by John Markham
Photographs by Patricia E. Deans

ACKNOWLEDGEMENTS

Assistance towards the compilation and the costs of this publication has generously been provided by:
The Elston family of Letwell; Mrs. S. W. Halkyard; Mrs. S. M. Jefferson of Brandesburton; Mrs. J. C. Kelly of Cherry Burton; Dr. C. Plowman of Knaresborough; Mrs. J. Precious of Grimsby; Mrs. K. Punter of Gosforth; Mrs. J. L. Shannon of Edinburgh; Mrs. J. B. Smith; and Mrs. V. Wood of Cottingham in memory of the late Frank Charles Wood.

This publication would not have been possible without the generous assistance of those people and institutions who have provided the originals from which the plates were made. The Society wishes to thank Beverley Borough Council and St. Mary's Church, Beverley, Mr. and Mrs. G. Barton; and relatives of T. B. Burton *viz* the families of Burton, Halkyard, Harrison, Jefferson, Plowman, Precious, Smith and Sutherby, for the loan of material from their private collections. Many people have helped with identifications of subjects; we are particularly grateful to E. J.Hobson, Berna Moody and Roy Wilson, and to Alan Williamson for his contribution on Burton the artist.

THOMAS BONFREY BURTON (1866-1941)

by

John Markham

Thomas Bonfrey Burton was born at 41 Freehold Street, Hull, on 10 March 1866, the eldest of the eight children of John Burton (1840-1922), whose father Thomas Burton (1808-1886) was a boot- and shoe-maker at 55 Saturday Market. John Burton was apprenticed to a Beverley joiner, but moved to Hull and became a builder.

T. B. Burton took a deep interest in his ancestry and descendants, neatly recording in the family Bible all the facts he could discover. Through his three time great-grandfather, Edward Bonfrey, who had married a Mary Tennison, he had a distant link with Alfred, Lord Tennyson: they shared a common ancestor, Michael Tennisonne, who was born in Keyingham in 1663.

After a short period as a teacher for Hull School Board, T. B. Burton returned to Beverley to become an apprentice to his uncle, Thomas Loft, a house painter and picture frame-maker, whose premises were at 23 Toll Gavel. Painting and decorating provided an inadequate outlet for Burton's artistic talent, and he paid tribute to the kindness of Thomas Loft who, at a time when the young man was finding his ordinary work rather 'tame', enabled him to have lessons from James Burras, an elderly local artist. In 1887 he was made Loft's partner, then took sole charge of the business from 1888 until 1897, when he and his younger brother, William Bastow Burton (known as Will), became partners in the firm, thereafter called Burton Brothers.

Burton Brothers was a very successful business and, as the only large contractors in the area, undertook high quality contract work, decorating many important houses and other large buildings in Beverley and the surrounding area, among them Bar House, the Barracks, the Sessions House, Bishop Burton Hall, Dalton Hall, the Minster and St. Mary's Church, where a major undertaking, completed in the early days of the Second World War, was the restoration of the chancel ceiling.

The two brothers are still held in high regard by those who knew them. One former employee who became, in 1921 when he was 13, an apprentice in the firm at a weekly wage of 4s. 6d. has stated that they were 'the best bosses anyone could ever have worked for'. He recalls Tom Burton as a refined and dignified man who supervised his men but never did any manual work himself. Will, however, did all the graining, then so fashionable, and put the finishing touches to outside work. Though a very private man, T. B. Burton's independence enabled him to stand firm and defy critics when circumstances so demanded; such a situation occurred when he decided to employ Frederick Fairfield, an experienced painter from the shipyard but not a member of a union, and all the Burton workmen declared they would strike rather than accept a non-union colleague. Tom Burton refused to budge, and the threatened industrial action evaporated.

The two Burton brothers differed in temperament, but worked well together, and even lived as next-door neighbours at houses in Woodlands, Beverley, which their father John had built. Later in life, the attic of 16 Woodlands, where T. B. Burton lived with his wife and three children, was converted into a studio; it was there, in the limited time he could spare from his business and family responsibilities, that he devoted himself to art. He was particularly skilful at producing etchings and worked with great precision, transferring his original pencil drawings to copper plates.

The 1880s were a prolific period when, as a young man completing his apprenticeship and under James Burras's tuition, Burton drew a number of Beverley buildings, some of neat Georgian appearance, soon to be demolished or replaced by others in styles more acceptabie to Victorian taste. The imminent demise of much that was familiar resulted in a valuable historical

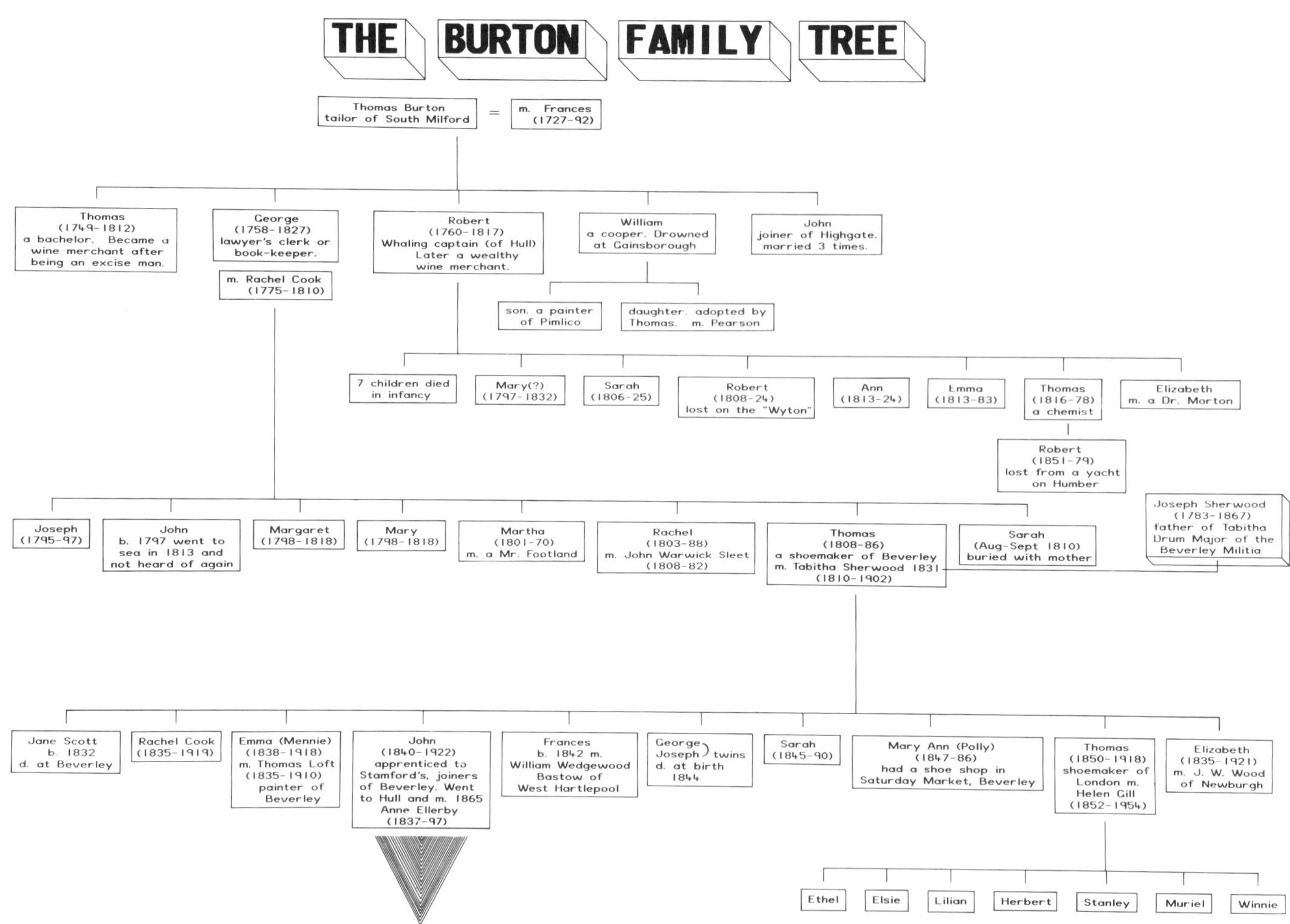
THE BURTON FAMILY TREE
Thomas Burton tailor of South Milford
m. Frances (1727-92)
Thomas (1749-1812) a bachelor. Became a wine merchant after being an excise man.
George (1758-1827) lawyer's clerk or book-keeper.
m. Rachel Cook (1775-1810)
Robert (1760-1817) Whaling captain (of Hull) Later a wealthy wine merchant.
William a cooper. Drowned at Gainsborough
John joiner of Highgate. married 3 times.
son. a painter of Pimlico
daughter. adopted by Thomas. m. Pearson
7 children died in infancy
Mary(?) (1797-1832)
Sarah (1806-25)
Robert (1808-24) lost on the "Wyton"
Ann (1813-24)
Emma (1813-83)
Thomas (1816-78) a chemist
Elizabeth m. a Dr. Morton
Robert (1851-79) lost from a yacht on Humber
Joseph Sherwood (1783-1867) father of Tabitha Drum Major of the Beverley Militia
Joseph (1795-97)
John b. 1797 went to sea in 1813 and not heard of again
Margaret (1798-1818)
Mary (1798-1818)
Martha (1801-70) m. a Mr. Footland
Rachel (1803-88) m. John Warwick Sleet (1808-82)
Thomas (1808-86) a shoemaker of Beverley m. Tabitha Sherwood 1831 (1810-1902)
Sarah (Aug-Sept 1810) buried with mother
Jane Scott b. 1832 d. at Beverley
Rachel Cook (1835-1919)
Emma (Mennie) (1838-1918) m. Thomas Loft (1835-1910) painter of Beverley
John (1840-1922) apprenticed to Stamford's, joiners of Beverley. Went to Hull and m. 1865 Anne Ellerby (1837-97)
Frances b. 1842 m. William Wedgewood Bastow of West Hartlepool
George Joseph twins d. at birth 1844
Sarah (1845-90)
Mary Ann (Polly) (1847-86) had a shoe shop in Saturday Market, Beverley
Thomas (1850-1918) shoemaker of London m. Helen Gill (1852-1954)
Elizabeth (1835-1921) m. J. W. Wood of Newburgh
Ethel
Elsie
Lilian
Herbert
Stanley
Muriel
Winnie

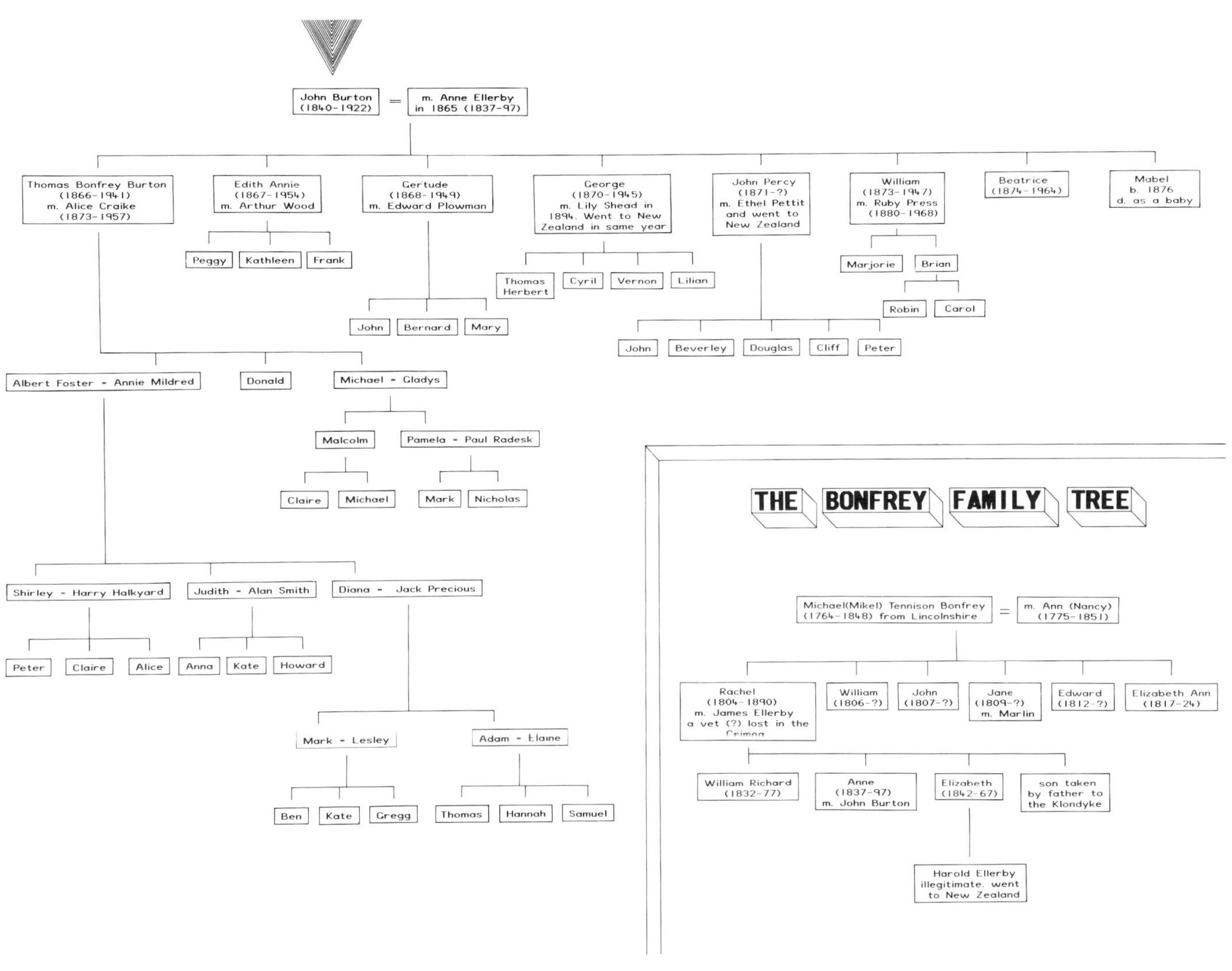
John Burton (1840-1922)
m. Anne Ellerby in 1865 (1837-97)
Thomas Bonfrey Burton (1866-1941) m. Alice Craike (1873-1957)
Edith Annie (1867-1954) m. Arthur Wood
Gertude (1868-1949) m. Edward Plowman
George (1870-1945) m. Lily Shead in 1894. Went to New Zealand in same year
John Percy (1871-?) m. Ethel Pettit and went to New Zealand
William (1873-1947) m. Ruby Press (1880-1968)
Beatrice (1874-1964)
Mabel b. 1876 d. as a baby
Peggy
Kathleen
Frank
John
Bernard
Mary
Thomas Herbert
Cyril
Vernon
Lilian
John
Beverley
Douglas
Cliff
Peter
Marjorie
Brian
Robin
Carol
Albert Foster - Annie Mildred
Donald
Michael - Gladys
Malcolm
Pamela - Paul Radesk
Claire
Michael
Mark
Nicholas
Shirley - Harry Halkyard
Judith - Alan Smith
Diana - Jack Precious
Peter
Claire
Alice
Anna
Kate
Howard
Mark - Lesley
Adam - Elaine
Ben
Kate
Gregg
Thomas
Hannah
Samuel
THE BONFREY FAMILY TREE
Michael(Mikel) Tennison Bonfrey (1764-1848) from Lincolnshire
m. Ann (Nancy) (1775-1851)
Rachel (1804-1890) m. James Ellerby a vet (?) lost in the Crimea
William (1806-?)
John (1807-?)
Jane (1809-?) m. Marlin
Edward (1812-?)
Elizabeth Ann (1817-24)
William Richard (1832-77)
Anne (1837-97) m. John Burton
Elizabeth (1842-67)
son taken by father to the Klondyke
Harold Ellerby illegitimate. went to New Zealand

Thomas Bonfrey Burton as a young man.

Burton Family Group

The photograph shows, front, T. B. Burton's grandmother Tabitha Burton, née Sherwood (1810-1902), who in 1831 had married TBB's grandfather, Thomas (1808-1886), a Beverley shoemaker. Behind are two of their children, TBB's aunt Mary Ann, known as Polly (1847-1886) and his uncle Thomas (1850-1918), a shoemaker in London. Tabitha, born in the reign of George III, was one of the earliest Beverley-born people ever to be photographed.

record, although in his later work he moved away from visual documentation to subjects selected more for their intrinsic artistic quality. Yet all his work reveals him as a sensitive and gentle man with a love of beauty and tranquillity.

Burton's sketches, etchings and paintings demonstrate the extent of his range and the quantity and quality of his artistic output. 'Incredibly modest, for so gifted a man,' wrote an obituarist in the *Beverley Guardian* of 1941, 'his pleased yet deprecating smile when artists complimented him was an indication of a lovable character.' Fred Elwell, his contemporary, who was not a man disposed to lavish praise on fellow artists, stated that Burton had the talent to make his living as an artist if circumstances had been different.

T. B. Burton exhibited his work locally and sold his etchings in the Toll Gavel shop for modest prices — £1 to £2 according to size. He was a well-respected member of the community, but he shunned the limelight and it was not until an exhibition of work in the Beverley Art Gallery in 1991, on the anniversary of his death, that he received some measure of the greater public recognition he deserved. The interest aroused by that exhibition led to a desire to produce a more permanent record of his work, and the East Yorkshire Local History Society has given expression to that wish by publishing the present volume.

Thomas Burton's Boot and Shoe Shop.

T. B. Burton's grandfather, also Thomas, was a boot- and shoemaker at 55 Saturday Market, a 16th-century building with later additions, which was occupied at least into the early 1840s by Richard Clark Dossor, tailor and draper.

THOMAS BONFREY BURTON — THE ARTIST
by
Alan Williamson

Thomas Burton, whilst apparently receiving little formal art training, showed natural ability at an early age. It is possible that his apprenticeship to his uncle in the family painting and decorating business assisted his artistic development. In Victorian times, apprenticeship as a house painter and decorator lasted seven years. The young Thomas Burton would have been required to possess a knowledge of colour mixing and harmony, lettering, graining and marbling, and the principles of decorative art and perspective. Additionally, he would need to demonstrate freehand drawing, and his pen and ink sketches drawn in the 1880s may have been apprenticeship test pieces.

The family shop also sold artists' colours and carried out picture framing and gilding. This would have brought him into contact with other artists and their works. With this valuable background, he continued, in his limited spare time, to develop his artistic range, revealing an ability to paint and draw in any medium. He also became very skilled in the art of copper plate etching, mainly of local Beverley scenes. These were of a high standard, and copies sold readily from his Toll Gavel shop. Today they are among his best known works.

By the turn of the century his work started to reveal a greater awareness of architectural detail and perspective. He was equally at home with sea and landscape subjects; his versatility extended to still life, especially flower paintings, and to portraiture. Whilst not generally known for his figure paintings, the evidence contained in his pocket sketch-books show his competence to capture local life with the minimum use of line. Continuing themes in much of his work are night and moonlight. This shows the possible influence of J. Atkinson Grimshaw (1836-1893), the famous Leeds artist and master of nocturnal scenes. Burton's oil paintings of New Walk, St. Mary's Church, and Saturday Market (all illustrated in this volume) clearly demonstrate this point.

His close friendship with the better known Beverley artist, Fred Elwell R.A. (1870-1958), may well have been a further influence. Burton's first known paintings coincide with Elwell's return from Paris. Burton's landscapes and portraits show signs of the growing influence of the French Impressionist movement.

For a period of fifty years, Thomas Burton recorded for posterity, in his drawings and paintings, much of the town and countryside he loved. He was awarded the Silver Medal of the Beverley Photographic and Sketching Society in 1899. His works were also hung in both the Beverley and Hull Ferens art galleries. A generous man, he freely gave advice and encouragement to young artists; the 'New Walk' painting (reproduced in colour) was a wedding gift to one of his former pupils.

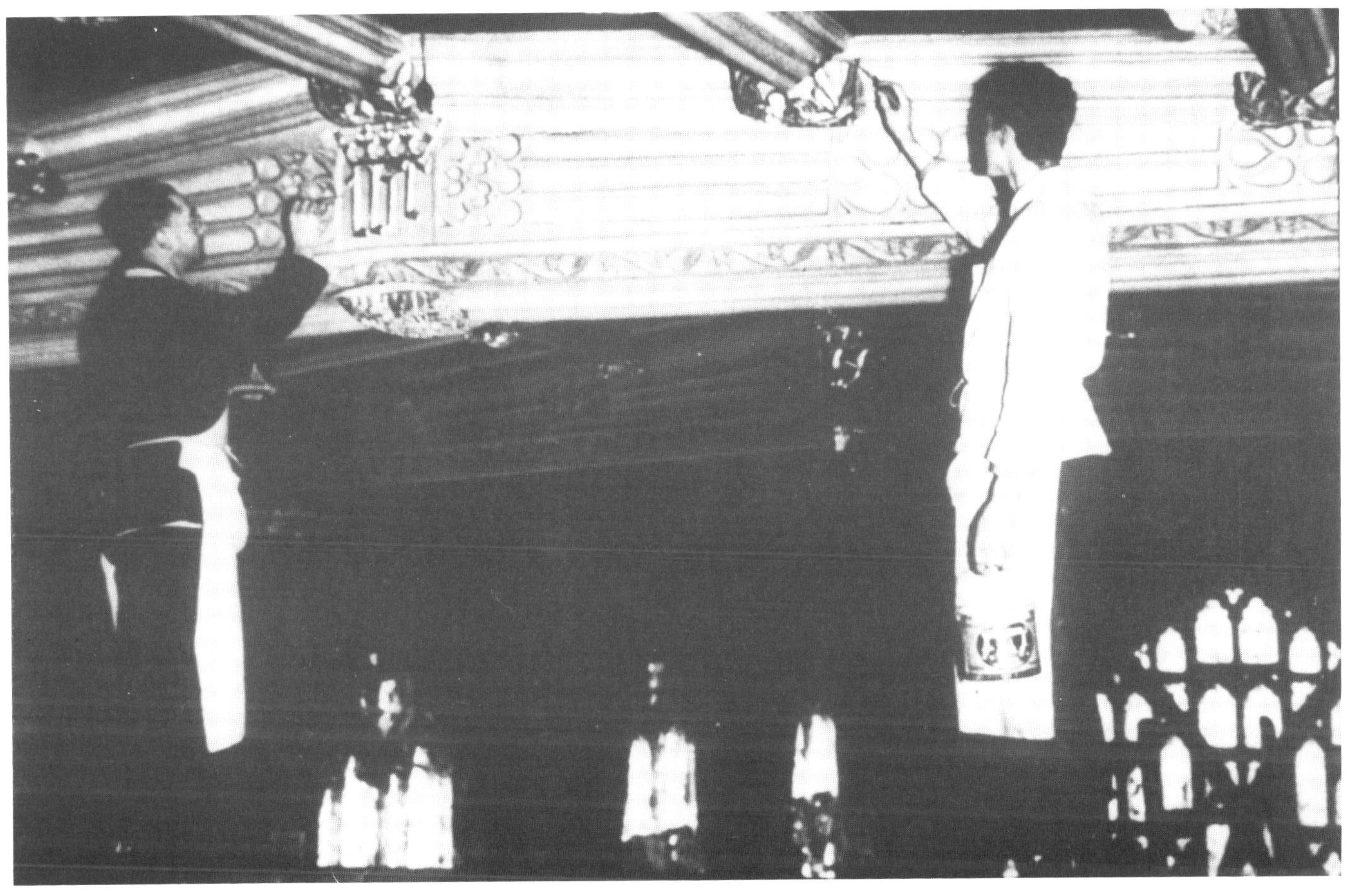

St. Mary's Church, Beverley.

One of Burton Brothers' important commissions was re-decoration of the ceiling of St. Mary's Church, 1936-1939. Most of the detailed work was done by their senior employee, John Cox.

BEVERLEY MINSTER TOWERS (c.1924)
The view of the west towers of the Minster from gardens which formerly occupied a large open area behind St. John Street and between Minster Moorgate and Keldgate, now the site of St. Matthew's Court. *Etching.*

BEVERLEY GRAMMAR SCHOOL (c.1886)

Burton's drawings of the exterior and interior of the Grammar School in Keldgate are examples of his visual record of buildings which were soon to disappear. The Keldgate building was erected 1816-17, next to No. 54, then occupied by the Grammar School Master, and replaced an earlier building in the south-west corner of the Minster churchyard. Although the school was successful during its early years in Keldgate, it suffered from financial problems and a declining number of pupils after 1842 when Beverley Corporation withdrew its support. It was closed in 1878 and demolished in 1890. Burton's ink drawing, made between closure and demolition, shows it as a simple neat building with Gothic-style windows and doorways, and the plain dual-flight wall staircase which led to the first-floor library at the rear has faint echoes of the sophisticated Chapter House staircase in the Minster. The contents of the room are presumably those left after closure: communal desks with benches, desks at which one stood to write, and the Master's dais. *Ink drawings.*

BEVERLEY GRAMMAR SCHOOL
(c.1886)

NO. 54 KELDGATE (c.1884)

No. 54 Keldgate has changed little in external appearance since Burton's drawing. Built c.1696 for the local landed family, the Constables, it became the residence of the Grammar School Master in the 1770s. Re-used 16th-century panelling and medieval remains formerly visible in the basement are indications of an earlier building on the site. From 1913 it was used as a boarding house for pupils at the Grammar School, which had re-opened in Queensgate in 1902. *Ink drawing.*

THE STONE DOG (1884)

Throughout Burton's life the so-called 'stone dog' stood outside 129 Keldgate, and it was customary for children to pat it as they passed to and from school. No one is certain of its origin and, as Burton's ink drawing shows, it was already well-worn with few features remaining on its face in 1884. Berna Moody, who has investigated its history, noted that No. 129 Keldgate has large stone quoins of magnesian limestone, probably taken from an earlier building and perhaps the previous location of the 'dog', which is made of similar material. The house in Keldgate is not far from the site of the demolished Keldgate Bar and St. Thomas's chapel, and either of these could have been the earlier location of the stonework.

Berna Moody also observed that the carving had webbed feet and evidence of scales, indications that it could have been a 'sea-dog', the early heraldic artists' attempt to depict a beaver, the symbol of Beverley. The stone dog is now in the garden of the Dominican Friary as the gift of Mr. T. A. Layard. *Ink drawing.*

FOX'S HOSPITAL (1884)
Fox's Hospital in Minster Moorgate was an almshouse founded by Thwaites Fox in 1636 to provide accommodation for four poor widows. It was closed in 1872 and Burton made his sketch in 1884 shortly before its demolition. *Ink drawing.*

No. 58 FLEMINGATE (1884)

No. 58 Flemingate, is according to tradition, the birthplace of St. John Fisher, Bishop of Rochester, who was executed in 1535 for his refusal to accept Henry VIII as supreme Head of the Church in England. Two facts, however, do not support this belief. The house, built in brick and an example of Artisan Mannerism (the individualistic use of classical features by a local craftsman) dates from the late 17th century, long after John Fisher's death. His father, Robert, a merchant, was a benefactor of St. Mary's Church, where he was buried, and this would not be the local church for a man living at the southern end of the town. This, nevertheless, is inconclusive evidence, and it is possible that the 17th century house replaced an earlier one. *Ink drawing.*

THE FRIARY (1884)

The Dominican Friary was founded before 1240, though the surviving section was a re-building following a fire in 1449. After dissolution in 1539, the Friary passed into private ownership, and was subdivided in the 19th century. Throughout Burton's lifetime the Friary was divided into three houses, and his etching shows the middle house, for a long time occupied by the Woodmansey family, and particularly by Miss Annie Woodmansey, a washerwoman of great repute and character, who remained there until her final illness in 1964. In 1960 the Friary was bought by Armstrong Patents Ltd. Permission to demolish was refused, and restoration began in 1974. It was opened as a Youth Hostel in 1980. *Etching.*

EASTGATE (1888)

These old houses at the northern end of Eastgate adjoined the Railway Tavern, opened at the south-east corner of Wednesday Market after the coming of the railway to Beverley in 1846. In 1881 the innkeeper was Eleanor Boulton. The half-timbered houses had a central passage entrance to the rear but should not be confused with the still surviving rear entrance to The Monk's Walk, formerly the George and Dragon, which is further south in Eastgate. Other houses were later built on the site of those drawn by TBB, and the Railway Tavern has been demolished, with its site left vacant. *Ink drawing.*

RAILWAY STREET/EASTGATE (1887)
The house at the junction of Railway Street (left) and Eastgate (right) was a private residence at the time of Burton's ink drawing.

In the early 1800s it appears to have been the home of John Wilkinson Crathorne, miller. By 1909, as Burton's annotation shows (lower right corner), it had been converted into the premises of N. J. Gray, grocer, although the broad parapet above the first-floor windows then bore in large letters the name 'Geo F. Burton Ltd'.

By 1892 a mock-Tudor porch (just visible in the sketch) had been erected at the corner of the building, and after many years as a shop it became the Tudor Rose restaurant. *Ink drawing.*

WEDNESDAY MARKET/RAILWAY STREET/ EASTGATE (1892)
A photograph of c.1860 in Philip Brown's *Old Beverley* (plate 32) indicates that the buildings in Wednesday Market (left) had been altered since that date and before Burton made this ink drawing in 1892. In a subsequent alteration the unassuming house and shop depicted by Burton were to be replaced by two more imposing Victorian shops with large plate-glass windows on the ground floor, shallow bow windows on the first floor, Dutch gables, and dormer windows in the tiled roof. The premises were occupied by W. H. Sugdon, bookseller and stationer (left) and Edwin Hayman (chemist). *Ink drawing.*

NO. 16 BUTCHER ROW (1884)

No. 16 Butcher Row was built c.1769, possibly by William Middleton, who played a major role in the Georgianisation of Beverley and who was responsible for the Guildhall, the Assembly Rooms, the Beverley Arms and a number of houses as well as the now demolished Fish Shambles. Index, the bookshop, now occupies the building in Butcher Row, and, although the ground floor has been completely altered, the upper frontage remains virtually unchanged. In 1881 it appears to have been occupied by Edmund Crosskill, an agricultural engineer employing 90 men, and son of William Crosskill, founder of the engineering firm which had enjoyed spectacular success until bankers foreclosed in the mid-Victorian period. In 1891 it was apparently occupied by Henry Brown, butcher. *Ink drawing.*

BUTCHER ROW (1884)

Another sketch indicating the considerable changes made to the appearance of Beverley at the turn of the century. The typical Georgian shop window of Alfred Isott (or Issott), painter, 4 Butcher Row, and the low first-floor window (possibly a Yorkshire casement), which survived in 1884, were to be replaced by 1905 by a grand plate-glass ground-floor frontage, with a four-paned sash window above. The shuttered Georgian sash windows of the adjoining house (No. 2) were also removed. Burton has annotated his drawing to record the changes of occupiers. Issott's (No. 4) was then the premises of Benjamin Nicholson, fishmonger, and George Riby, painter (No. 2) , had been succeeded by another painter, Robert Campey. *Ink drawing.*

LAIRGATE CHAPEL (undated)

Burton has made another record of a long-demolished Georgian building, replaced by a more ornate Victorian successor which in turn has been demolished. He has depicted the Independent (or Congregationalist) Chapel built in Lairgate in 1800 on the site of a former Presbyterian Chapel. He notes (with obvious signs of uncertainty) the date of demolition, 1881, probably a few years out as the Victorian replacement was built 1886-7. That was closed in 1976 and three 'town houses' (Nos. 74A-C) now occupy the site. *Ink drawing.*

THE CORN EXCHANGE (1884)

In 1824 the Corn Exchange drawn by Burton had been converted from the front section of the Butchers' Shambles built in 1753 by Samuel Smith in the northern part of Saturday Market known as Corn Hill. Burton again has captured an important public building at the end of its life: in 1886 the red-brick Corn Exchange replaced the more modest Georgian building. In 1911 it became the Picture Playhouse. *Ink drawing*.

SITE OF THE SHAMBLES (1886)

A rare and probably unique picture of the site in Saturday Market where butchers had their stalls from at least 1600 and where permanent Butchers' Shambles were erected in 1753. The rear section of this Georgian building was converted into a Corn Exchange in 1825, with a Butter Market incorporated in 1834.

Burton's picture shows this traditional trading area cleared of buildings to provide space for the new Corn Exchange and Butter Market, opened in 1886, and the Baths, opened in 1887. *Ink drawing.*

NEW WALK/MOLESCROFT ROAD (1892)
New Walk, developed in the 18th century as a fashionable promenade, retained its rural appearance well into the 19th century, and Molescroft Road was still sparsely populated until the building of houses in the 1920s and 1930s. Burton's fascination with the effect of light is beautifully conveyed in this picture, entitled 'After a Rainy Day', which shows New Walk viewed from a point near St. Mary's Cemetery in Molescroft Road. *Oil painting.*

NO. 16 WOODLANDS (1923)

The inside of 16 Woodlands, the home of T. B. Burton, where he had his attic studio. The house and that of his brother, Will, next door (No. 18), had been built by their father, John. The interior, a rare subject for TBB, recalls the paintings of domestic scenes within Bar House and other Beverley buildings made by Burton's contemporary, Fred Elwell. *Oil painting.*

OLD SHOP IN WALKERGATE (c.1913)

Burton was attracted by the sight of a lit building spreading its glow into the gloom of night, and as an experiment produced this coloured etching of an old shop in Walkergate. The shop, on the west side, was demolished as part of modern road developments which included the building of the Sow Hill bus station. *Oil painting.*

ST. MARY'S CHURCH BY MOONLIGHT
St. Mary's church seen from the west end, across the street in North Bar Within. A typical Burton scene, of a building casting its light into the gloom of a winter's night. *Oil painting.*

STANDING AT THE SITTINGS (undated)

The hirings, or sittings, when farm workers and servants offered themselves in the streets for a year's employment, were held on 6 and 11 November. The first occasion followed Ringing Day Fair, and the second was the result of Beverley's adherence to the original date of Martinmas, which had officially moved to 23 November when eleven days were 'lost' after the reform of the calendar in 1752. As the only holiday most employees enjoyed, they were always lively and sometimes disorderly occasions when the many colourful characters and incidents on view provided abundant material for an artist's sketch-book. The hirings still functioned as a labour market in the 1920s, but by the 1930s they survived merely as social events. *Notebook, pencil sketch.*

TYMPERON'S HOSPITAL (1884)

Tymperon's Hospital, a neat Georgian building with the blind arcading so characteristic of Beverley, was founded as an almshouse by William Tymperon, whose will of 1729 left the manor of Aldbrough with two houses and 192 acres of land to enable a house to be purchased for six poor people. In 1953 it was sold. *Ink drawing.*

DOG KIRK GARTH (1884)

Burton's etching shows an old building on the southern side of Norwood known for some inexplicable reason as Dog Kirk Garth, but also as Porche House (*sic*). The home of the Jude family, it was demolished in the later years of the war. Clock Service Garage now occupies the site of the house, which stood beside the building in which the Beverley Music Centre is now located. *Etching.*

NO. 17-23 NORTH BAR WITHIN (1886)

T. B. Burton's ink drawing of shops in North Bar Within, adjoining the entrance to Wood Lane, shows that many buildings retained their Georgian appearance well into the late Victorian period.

No. 17 North Bar Within, now occupied by Carmichael's of Beverley, was an 18th-century building, originally the town house of the Boyntons and later given a Victorian frontage by the architect, William Hawe. At the time of this drawing it was occupied by Charles Smithson, saddler and harness maker. No. 19, right of Wood Lane and now the premises of Wells Cundall, was built 1750 by the Wrightsons for a draper, Mr. Norris, and in 1886 was occupied by Henry Sugdon, grocer. No. 21 (now Robert Gail) was re-built by William Hawe soon after this drawing was made. In 1886 it was occupied by Robert Loftus, cabinet maker and upholsterer. No. 23 (now Murray Todd) is an 18th-century building, occupied in 1886 by John Malam, fruiterer. *Ink drawing.*

THE LAME COBBLER (undated)

'J. S.' is probably J. Sanderson, a cobbler in Wood Lane. *Pencil sketch.*

TIGER LANE (1881)

The building, left, is the northern end of the Tiger Inn, the Georgian rival of the nearby Beverley Arms for the status of Beverley's principal coaching inn. It was built c.1730 but had closed in 1847 after the opening of railways had a serious and ultimately fatal impact on the coaching trade. After closure it was sub-divided into shops, and the section which abuts Tiger Lane (No. 47 North Bar Within) was occupied in 1881 by John Hopper, plumber and upholsterer.

Tiger Lane was originally a private entrance to the extensive stables at the rear of the inn. A comparison with the sketch of c.1840 in Philip Brown's *Old Beverley*, plate 81, shows that a gate had been removed, though part of the hinge survives.

The building to the right which is now the front part of St. Mary's Court (opened in 1982) had been much altered between c.1840 and 1881. (*Old Beverley*, plate 81). Burton's drawing shows new ground-floor and first-floor windows, dormer windows, and alteration to the central entrance. In 1881 these premises appear to have been occupied by Penelope Hoggard, dealer in Berlin wool, a type of thread used in worsted embroidery. In 1908 Gordon Armstrong opened a garage here. *Ink drawing.*

NORTH BAR WITHOUT: NOS 6 (right) and 8 (left) (1886)

Burton's ink drawing of North Bar Without at the junction of what is now Wylies Road (left) shows the Georgian house (No. 6) and shop (No. 8) before they were given their mock-Tudor appearance (1892-1894) by James E. Elwell, a woodcarver of considerable reputation, who also re-built his own premises (No. 4) in similar style. When transforming the appearance of No. 6 Elwell incorporated in the carving a record of their earlier appearance which corresponds with that in Burton's sketch. Elwell, however, placed the description, 'W. J. Thorley, Woodcarver', on the corner shop (No. 8).

This area contained the residence of Robert Wylie, J. P. and Deputy Lieutenant, c.1834—1894. After demolition of the house his name was commemorated by Wylies Road, created in 1960 from a lane known variously as Narrow Lane, Witty Lane, Wylie's Racket, Elwell's Racket, and, for reasons which need no explanation, Ticklebelly Alley. The houses in Wylies Road and Park Avenue are built on what had been Mr. Wylie's park land. Burton has updated his sketch with annotations showing Gordon R. Sanderson in Wylie's former house, and Thomas J. Bulman, saddler, in the re-built corner shop (No. 8). *Ink drawing.*

BLACK MILL (1931)

The Black Mill (with four sails), variously known as Westwood High Mill, Far Mill, and Burton's Mill, had been re-built in 1803, but was damaged by fire and dismantled in 1868, with only the tarred tower remaining. *Etching.*

WESTWOOD MILLS (c.1884)

The Westwood, over a long period, provided a convenient venue for military manoeuvres and assemblies of troops, and it was an obvious asset to the Barracks, opened in 1887, which made Beverley a military town. Burton, who was himself a part-time soldier in the Volunteer Training Corps during the First World War (the equivalent of the later Home Guard), sketched members of the Sheffield, Scarborough and Northallerton Rifle Volunteers at a summer camp: such joint camps were common.

Lawson's Mill, a five-sailed structure, was dismantled in 1891, leaving only the lower part. Burton's sketch pre-dates such demolition. The Anti-Mill was established in 1799 by the Union Mill Society which ran it as a co-operative venture in competition with the private mill owners who were accused of charging high prices. It ceased to be used c.1890 and the upper part with its five sails was dismantled, leaving the lower section which is now incorporated in the clubhouse of the Beverley and East Riding Golf Club.

In 1883 the Cardwell reforms converted the Rifle Volunteers into Volunteer Battalions. There was a transitional period while these changes were being effected, and evidence from the condition of the mills (above) suggests that Burton would make these sketches c.1884, a time when he was at his most active recording Beverley. *Pencil sketch.*

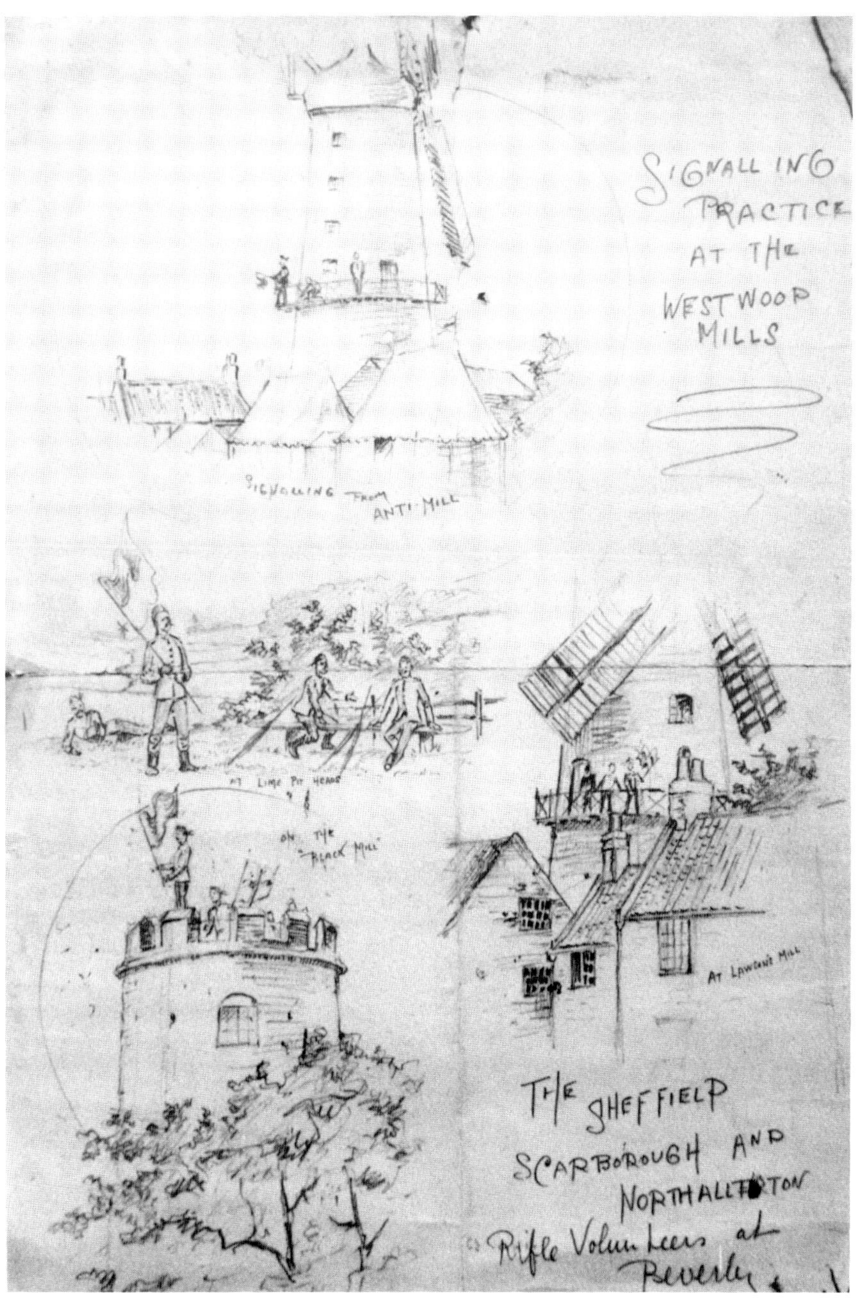

HUNTER'S SHIPYARD AT BEVERLEY LOCK (1925)

Shipbuilding, a traditional industry at Grovehill, received a boost with the spectacular growth of the Hull fishing industry and the introduction of steam-trawling in the late-19th century. A dry dock had been built by the lock in 1858, and in this drawing Burton shows the scene at Hunter's shipyard. Although it is a place of work, Burton is more attracted by the picturesque location and depicts it as a quiet backwater, with the gentle harmony of natural and man-made features which always caught his eye.

The Hunter family moved from Burton Stather to Beverley c.1898, and Joseph Hunter took over Thompson's shipyard (which he had previously managed) around 1912. Hunter's originally built and repaired barges; an incomplete barge in the yard in 1925 was not launched, because of the Depression, until 1938, when it was sold to the London & North-Eastern Railway Company for use in the Hull dock system. The yard produced lifeboats, for the Merchant Navy during the Second World War, and afterwards for Cook, Welton and Gemmell. The firm closed c.1956. *Etching.*

BECKSIDE (1934)

Beverley's close proximity to the River Hull and its links with the Humber and the North Sea made it a port with access to European markets, and a flourishing trading community with its own church of St. Nicholas developed in Beckside at the head of the canalised section known as Beverley Beck. In Burton's time, at the turn of the century, the Beck was still in commercial use, with keels regularly using its facilities, and here he captures the 'Dutch' atmosphere of the waterway and the pleasant groups of houses on its northern bank. *Etching.*

HULL BRIDGE (1912)

The bridge over the River Hull near Tickton was an important communication link between Beverley and the villages and coast beyond, and the road leading from the town and over the bridge was known as Holderness Road. Originally of wood, the bridge was re-built in stone by the late 14th century and, because of continual damage to its low structure, it was replaced by a higher bridge in 1803, forming an attractive feature and a convenient stopping place, with a riverside inn, the Crown and Anchor, nearby. Burton was to see the bridge he had drawn in 1912 replaced by a steel rolling bridge in 1913. This in turn was demolished, in 1976, and replaced by the present bridge. *Etching.*

BISHOP BURTON (1931)

An attractive part of a picturesque village. T. B. Burton has allowed himself a measure of artistic licence in order to show All Saints Church more fully than it would be seen from this angle, and to include the mid-19th-century cast-iron and wooden pump by the Mere. The house in the foreground, Mere Cottage, is little changed: the shutters on the window to the right of the door are no longer there. Many of the tall-chimneyed houses on the Bishop Burton estate are uncharacteristic of the East Riding, and there are stylistic similarities with Speke Hall, Cheshire, which Richard Watt bought in 1785, and with other houses in that area. A number of Bishop Burton houses with gables, dormer windows and sometimes half-timbering, were built or altered at the turn of the century by Ernest Richard Bradley Hall Watt (d.1908) and Richard Hall Watt (d.1918). *Etching.*

LECONFIELD (undated)

George Oliver described Leconfield in 1829 in the most enthusiastic terms: 'This village is placed in a romantic situation. The parkish appearance afforded to it by the taste and munificence of the noble family who made it their residence for so many centuries contributes much to heighten the general effect.' The Lords of the Manor were the Percy family who originally occupied a castle there. It was demolished in the 17th century but the archives at Petworth House, the Sussex residence of Baron Leconfield, indicate that a number of plaster and thatch houses survived in the village in 1811. Burton's sketch shows that they were still there many years later and it was clearly their artistic rather than their historical interest which appealed to him. It is a picture of gentle, unhurried decay, appealing to a man who shunned the limelight and preferred the quiet corners of life. *Pencil sketch.*

CHALK PITS (1925)
One of the benefits to Beverley of the Westwood was its provision of chalk, and a chalk quarry and limekilns were in use from the 14th century. Prisoners in the East Riding House of Correction off New Walk had to work the treadmill which crushed chalk for the manufacture of whiting. An 1840 directory states: 'Near Chalk Villa on the Queensgate or Hessle Road [re-named Victoria Road following the opening of the barracks in 1887] are two excellent chalk quarries of which the best whiting is made, and imbedded in the stone are the fossil impressions of shells, bones etc.' *Etching.*

CHALK VILLA (undated)

One of Burton's most sophisticated works is this etching of Chalk Villa, which stands on the west side of the present Victoria Road in the area on the outer edge of the town known as Beverley Parks. Set back from the road and approached by a drive, it originally occupied a very rural setting.

Built 1835-9 for William Brown, an army commissary, it was situated in Stone Pit Close, not far from the chalk pits which no doubt provided the chalk blocks used in its construction. In 1879 it was occupied by Joseph Goodfellow. *Etching.*

WATTON ABBEY (1926)

Burton had an eye for the artistic composition created by a tall building surrounded by trees and viewed in profile from an interesting angle. His etching of the prior's house of what is known as Watton Abbey (though, correctly, Watton Priory) shows, like so much of his work, his feeling for places of peace and tranquillity and his appreciation of their serenity.

An Anglo-Saxon nunnery at Watton (Wetadun), the scene of a miracle performed by St. John of Beverley and recorded by Bede, was replaced by the Gilbertine Priory of St. Mary c.1150 which followed the rule of Gilbert of Sempringham, founder of the one religious order of English origin, and which accommodated both men and women: a community of nuns and a quite separate establishment of canons to officiate at their services.

Watton was dissolved in 1539-40 and the prior's lodging, converted into a house, has for centuries been owned by members of the Bethell family. *Etching.*

ST. NICHOLAS CHURCH, HORNSEA (1919)
A 13th-century church restored 1865-7 by Sir George Gilbert Scott. This view is from the garden of the Old Hall. *Etching.*

SOUTHGATE, HORNSEA (undated)
Information supplied by Hornsea local historian, Mr. E. J. Hobson, identifies this as the view northwards towards the town centre. The tall building (left) is the gable end of Low Hall (better known as The White House or Harker's Farm). The buildings in front are the farm buildings, and the entrance to the farm yard is between them. The 'medallion' on the gable (front) was a sign erected by the Automobile Association, giving the mileages from Hornsea to various places. The cottages (right) have been demolished and the site is now occupied by the Catholic Church. *Etching.*

SEATON ROAD, HORNSEA (undated)

T. B. Burton identified this scene as 'Seaton Road, Hornsea', the attractive entrance to the town, which crosses what was once common land and which recalls a rural past which was even more evident in his day. The Burton family owned property in Hornsea, and Burton had relations living there. His affection for the area is proved by the number of times Hornsea featured in his work. In spite of Burton's own identification of this view, it is the opinion of the Hornsea local historian, Mr. E. J. Hobson, that the etching is of the west end of Eastgate and that the building in the centre is White Cottage, which still survives and which has particular interest as the house where the then owner, Wing Commander Sims, entertained 'Aircraftsman Shaw' — Lawrence of Arabia. *Etching.*

BEN TILLETT (1893)

Ben Tillett, Secretary of the Dockers' Union and leader of a successful dock strike in London in 1889, was in Hull on a number of occasions in the period 1889-93 when unemployment was growing and there was conflict between employers and dock workers, who were becoming increasingly unionised. Antagonism culminated in the bitter and violent dock strike of 1893 when C. H. Wilson, Liberal M.P. and effective head of the largest shipping company, Thomas Wilson & Sons, refused to abandon the practice of giving preferential employment to non-union dockers.

Corporation Field, Park Street, then used as a wholesale fruit and vegetable market, earlier by Hull Fair and later by the horse fair, was the traditional venue for mass meetings such as the one addressed by Tillett on Thursday, 6 April 1893, the day when the strike began. It ended after six weeks in total defeat for the dockers. *Pencil sketch.*

HIGH STREET, HULL (1921)

Burton did little drawing in Hull, and this etching of High Street has particular interest because of its date, 1921, when it still maintained its traditional role as a centre for businesses connected with water transport. High Street in 1921 contained a number of buildings of considerable age, some half-timbered and with jettied storeys, which were to be destroyed in the Second World War or later demolished.

The sketch shows, far left, the wall of Wilberforce House (No. 25) and, near left, what are now the Georgian Houses, part of the Wilberforce House complex (No. 24) but in 1921 the premises of J. De Paiva & Co., sack merchants, and R. Grainger & Son, lighter owners. Near right is the entrance to Holden's Terrace; opposite No. 24, the Telegraph and Messengers Christian Association Institute (No. 179); the entrance to Bryant's Court (not visible); opposite Wilberforce House, C. Ware & Sons, water-proof cover and blind makers (No. 178) and John Good and Sons Ltd, ships' chandlers (Nos. 176 and 177); Ash & King, printers (No. 175); Thomas Scott, joiner (No. 174); George Yard (not visible). *Etching.*